It's **NEVER Too Late** & You're **NEVER Too Old**

---

50 PEOPLE WHO FOUND
SUCCESS AFTER 50

VIC JOHNSON

Laurenzana Press

Published by:
Laurenzana Press
PO Box 1220
Melrose, FL 32666 USA

www.LaurenzanaPress.com

ISBN-13: 978-1-937918-78-1

CONTENTS

INTRODUCTION

TRIALS AND TRIBULATIONS THAT PRECEDE SUCCESS

"One has to remember that every failure can be a stepping-stone to something better…"

~Harland "The Colonel" Sanders

Harland Sanders experienced a very difficult life as a child. He was born into poverty, his father died when he was young, and after his mother remarried he was severely beaten by his stepfather. Needing to escape the abuse, he went to live with his uncle.

Wanting a better life, he falsified his date of birth to enlist in the U.S. Army. After he was honorably discharged, he moved to Alabama and tried to have the quality of life he didn't have as a child. He married Josephine King in 1908, started a family, and was holding down a steady job. But things weren't in the stars for him to have the dream life he had hoped for.

While he was away on a business trip his wife gave away all their belongings, moved back to her parents' home, and divorced him. He was told by his ex-brother-in-law, "She had no business marrying a no-good fellow like you who can't hold a job."

Over the years Sanders had many jobs including steamboat pilot, streetcar conductor, insurance salesman, railroad fireman,

1

farmer, and service station operator. Then in the midst of the Great Depression he bravely opened a gas station and small restaurant named Sanders Court & Café where he served family style meals. His popularity grew, and he moved the restaurant into a much larger site where he worked on a recipe for pressure cooker chicken that cooked much faster than being fried.

Things were beginning to look up for this tenacious man from Indiana. People were coming from all over for his famous chicken. Duncan Hines listed his restaurant in "Adventures in Good Eating." He got remarried in 1949, and was given the moniker of "Kentucky Colonel" by Governor Lawrence Wetherby.

Having already established his "brand" with his white suit, black tie, shock-white hair and beard, he drove around in his Cadillac with his face painted on the side. Going from town to town, he finally meets Pete Harman in Salt Lake City, and awards him the first franchise. In return, he was to be paid five cents for every piece of chicken sold.

But in 1955, another dark cloud hovered over his life when an interstate was built near his restaurant that deflected over 75% of his clientele. At the age of 65 (when most people are retiring) he closed his doors and found himself flat broke.

The one and only thing the Colonel had left in his arsenal was his famous chicken recipe. He believed in it so much that he sold his gas station, took his first Social Security check, and went on the road to sell the recipe to restaurants.

As they say, the rest is history. By 1964 there were over 600 Colonel Sanders Kentucky Fried Chicken franchises in the U.S., Canada and England. Although Sanders sold his interest in the company for $2 million, he continued to work until he died in 1980 from leukemia. The gallant Kentucky Colonel was 90 years old.

Potential entrepreneurs can find hope in the story of a man who at the age of 65 could have easily given up and retired. It's been said that Sanders was turned down more than 1,000 times during his attempts to succeed at an age when most people would have retired.

The trials and tribulations of tackling such an ambitious goal is the inspiration behind his success. Perseverance, belief in his product, and an unwillingness to give up is what drove the Colonel to ultimate fame and fortune.

Overcoming Obstacles

"As soon as a man recognizes that he has drifted into age, he gets reminiscent. He wants to talk and talk; and not about the present or the future, but about his old times. For there is where the pathos of his life lies – and the charm of it. The pathos of it is there because it was opulent with treasures that are gone, and the charm of it is in casting them up from the musty ledgers and remembering how rich and gracious they were."

~"FRANK FULLER AND MY FIRST NEW YORK LECTURE,"
PUBLISHED IN 2009 IN WHO IS MARK TWAIN?

"It's never too late to be who you might have been."
~GEORGE ELIOT, 19TH CENTURY ENGLISH NOVELIST

The difference between these two quotes is a person can reminisce about their life, or they can live it to the fullest until their last breath. This book was written to show you how to prevent obstacles that could keep you from living your dreams.

3

One of the biggest hurdles people over 50 have to overcome is the mindset about their age. There's an old cliché of "age ain't nothin' but a number." But as we all know, getting older does have certain obstacles such as dwindling health, limited income, and the end of long-time careers followed by "now what in the heck do I do?"

Yes, age is the number of candles on a birthday cake, and a stark reality of things to come. But getting older isn't...

...a deal breaker.

...a reason you can't start a business.

...a limit on success.

...a valid excuse for inaction.

...a valid excuse to give up on your dreams.

There are older people who are young, and young people who are old. Many obstacles are self-inflicted and imaginary, and many are real. So you've got to decide if your dreams are worth the challenge of overcoming your obstacles (and you also need to figure out if they really exist, or just ones you've built out of fear).

To be honest, your age is an obstacle only if you allow it to be. If you're as tenacious as Colonel Sanders when you're 65, it shouldn't even be an issue.

The Best Years of My Life

Like Colonel Sanders I had some success early in my life, and achieved things I was quite proud of. For one, I became somewhat of a local legend in political circles where I rarely lost a campaign.

And like Sanders, I also had more than my share of failures. In fact, in my forties my family and I were evicted from our home, and a year later our last automobile was repossessed. I earned so little money that year that we qualified below the U.S. poverty level for a family of five.

The story of how I dug my way out is in some of my other books, so I won't belabor it here. But I do want to note that the very best years of my life came after I turned 50. Some of my achievements have been:

- Writing and publishing ten books, several of which became Amazon best sellers.

- Becoming a paid motivational speaker, speaking with some of the top names in the industry.

- Becoming a millionaire.

- Gaining international recognition as a goal-setting expert.

- Having my own television show.

When I was bogged down in my earlier struggles, I drew tremendous inspiration from many of the people highlighted in this book. Their examples of courage, dedication and tenacity proved to me that I wasn't washed up, and are the basis of *It's Never Too Late And You're Never Too Old*.

What You'll Get From My Book

We'll be looking at 50 examples of very successful people, including the illustrious Colonel Sanders, and you'll see that "success" means many different things.

Some are illustrations of powerful businesspeople whose success is measured in dollars and cents, and others who had a profound impact on history. Others simply made a difference to those around them. But there's one commonality they all share: Success came to all of them after they reached 50.

Some of these examples might reflect your current situation. They raised families, had good jobs, and had some early success with their dream, but set it aside due to obligations and what life handed them. But at the age of 50 or older, they found themselves longing for more. In *It's Never Too Late*, we will be discovering what "the more" is all about.

(Please pay attention to the Principle and Action at the end of each example, where they recap why that person was a success and how you can duplicate their efforts.)

Whatever age you might be, and whatever obstacles you may have to overcome, I am giving you 50 reasons why **it's never too late and you're never too old** to live your dreams and find success!

(**Attention All Eagle Eyes**: We've had a number of people proof this book before we released it to you, but there is a chance you might spot something that was missed. If you find a typo or other obvious error, please send it to us. And if you're the first one to report it <u>we'll send you a free gift</u>! Send to: corrections@ laurenzanapress.com)

50 PEOPLE
WHO FOUND SUCCESS
AFTER 50

"I am aware that I am very old now; but I am also aware that I have never been so young as I am now, in spirit ... I am only able to perceive that I am old by a mental process; I am altogether unable to feel old in spirit. It is a pity, too, for my lapses from gravity must surely often be a reproach to me. When I am in the company of very young people I always feel that I am one of them, and they probably privately resent it."

~AUTOBIOGRAPHY OF MARK TWAIN, VOL. 2(2013), DICTATED OCTOBER, 30, 1906.

1

RICHARD ADAMS

B est known for his novel, *Watership Down*, Richard Adams is an archetypical "success after 50" story since his book wasn't published until he was 52 years old.

He had originally come up with the story about rabbits for his daughters during long trips. (Simple stories told to children that are then turned into books is quite common. Take, for instance, Lewis Carroll who wrote *Alice in Wonderland* for Hendry Lindell's daughters).

Adams had been a British Civil Servant for 24 years by the time Rex Collings (after several rejections by other publishers) agreed to publish his novel.

Immediately achieving national and international acclaim, *Watership Down* (which was made into a movie in 1978) has sold over 50 million copies across the globe. Needless to say, it's a good thing the author's daughters convinced him to write the novel.

Adams wrote over 20 works during his late-in-life years as a writer. Born in England in 1920, he's still penning pieces such as *Gentle Footprints* (short story, "Leopard Aware" in a charity book for The Born Free Foundation).

Principle:

Richard Adams had a story spinning in his head for some time. But it wasn't until he was prodded to write it did he take the time to hone it into the classic it is today. Even though it was difficult to spend two years on a project only to have it constantly rejected, his tenacity (and some well-placed timing) brought his project to fruition. The point to this is if you don't give up, the journey isn't over.

Action:

Everyone has stories to tell, but few actually take action to get them down on paper. What poignant children's tale, or a fiction/non-fiction novel, is stored in the recesses of your mind? If there's one poking at you, it's probably time to sit down and write it. All it takes is one major effort (like Adams' *Watership Down*) to kick-start a career. **It's never too late** become the next Lewis Carroll, Richard Adams, or J. M. Barrie who wrote *Peter Pan*!

2

MICHAEL ALLEN

M any people think that being a successful athlete after the age of 50 isn't possible as they've become too old, and their bodies no longer can handle the sport.

Well, that's not necessarily true. Michael Allen debunked that theory by achieving great success in professional golf after turning 50.

Although Allen started playing mostly in international tournaments when he was 25 (he won the 1989 Scottish Open), he left the circuit in 1995 to focus on his family.

Then at the age of 53, he returned to the sport to secure a number of top three finishes on the Senior Championship Tour (the "senior circuit" for pros and amateurs over the age of 48). As the *New York Times* wrote, "Allen is defeating many of the same players who used to whip him regularly."

Of course golf isn't football, basketball, or any of the harsher sports as it's less demanding on the body. Nevertheless, Michael Allen's success shows that athletic success *can* be achieved after the age of 50.

Principle:

Success doesn't have to be just a state of mind since the body can also experience success. Michael Allen is an example of someone who became excelled at a physical activity rather than becoming sedentary and too old to move. You need to remember his story whenever you think your body is too old to participate in sports.

Action:

Staying in the game of life (especially if it's a physical game) will ultimately determine your success. Just because you haven't won before doesn't mean you can't start winning at the age of 50 or older. **It's never too late** to become the next Michael Allen!

3

MOMOFUKU ANDO

Just about every college student on a tight budget has subsisted on instant noodles. But they probably don't know about the man who invented them.

Although Momofuku Ando (1910-2007) followed his grandparent's footsteps by opening a textile business at 22, he ended up being famous for his Ramen noodles by the age of 50.

According to his biography, Ando had been providing "scholarships" for students. He was convicted for tax evasion in 1948 and spent two years in jail.

After losing his business due to bankruptcy, he founded Nissin Food Products (which started as a small family-run company producing salt).

Ando felt that noodles made with U.S. wheat would not be the way to feed the Japanese during post-WWII food shortages. He thought that mass-produced, easy-to-make and affordable noodles would have a greater chances of success (little did he know the success his noodles would eventually be back in the States).

At the age of 61, Ando had figured out the way to flash-fry the noodles, and started selling his Cup Noodle (*Kappu Nūdoru*) in a waterproof polystyrene container. The product originally had a high price point, but when the price was lowered the noodles took off and Ando had a hit on his hands. Due to his success in aiding the Japanese economy, he was given many medals by his government and the Japanese emperor.

By the time he died in 2007, millions of people worldwide – including the United States that originally wanted the noodles to be made from its wheat – were eating his instant noodles.

Principle:

Momofuku Ando had started a business long before his invention of healthy, affordable noodles became a major hit. Sometimes a first business is successful, and provides a comfortable life to its founder. Sometimes success comes much later. But the important thing to remember is your first business doesn't have to be your last. You can start fresh, even with a concept as simple as instant noodles.

Action:

Ando used trial and error to come up with his invention. Because he never gave up on his idea of providing a food staple to his people, he became more successful than he could have ever dreamed. **It's never too late** to find the right "recipe" for your success!

4

ARTHUR S. BERGER

After serving in World War II, and retiring from his long career as a city attorney, Arthur Berger (1912-2003) switched the course of his life when he wrote several books about parapsychology (the power of the mind); a power he said is strong enough to slow the aging process.

Based on his own life, one would tend to agree with his theory. He wrote five books between the ages of 67 and 75 (and is still writing today, having released *What Nobody Knew: A Reincarnation Mystery* 2012). At 76 he was elected to political office, and at 80 he founded a project matching school kids with the elderly. Venturing out in yet another direction, he wrote and acted in a play at the age of 86.

Arthur was fascinated by the question of survival after physical death, and felt that as a lawyer he could analyze the evidence and determine what was valid and what was not. His *Lives and Letters in American Parapsychology* (1988) was described as "superb" by *Parapsychology Review*, and was selected by *Choice* for its "outstanding academic list."

As of this writing, Arthur continues to use his legal training as an Ombudsman for the State of Florida Department of Elder Affairs.

Principle:

Life can be amazingly abundant in opportunities if there are no pre-conceived notions about age limitations. You can stand in its way and prevent it from happening (people are their own self-sabotagers), or move out of the way and embrace possibilities. Arthur Berger never once allowed his age to get in the way of constant exploration of the mind (including his own).

Action:

If you've spent the better part of your life in a practical profession, try something on the creative plane (or vice versa). The switch in thought processes will keep your mind active, and if Arthur Berger's theories are correct it slows the aging process. It's never too late to let go of old notions and embrace fresh approaches!

5

HARRY BERNSTEIN

H arry Bernstein (1910-2011) was born in the United Kingdom, but eventually became renowned as an American writer. Up until his retirement at age 62 he had worked for movie production companies reading scripts, and as an editor for magazines such Popular Mechanics, Family Circle and Newsweek.

It wasn't an unsuccessful life by any means, but Bernstein's ambitions were even greater as he longed to write a great novel.

When Ruby (his wife of 67 years of marriage) died in 2002, Bernstein's loneliness inspired his memoir, The Invisible Wall: A Love Story That Broke Barriers. His first book (written when he was 93) covered details of his life such as his mother, Ada, struggling to feed her six children; an abusive alcoholic feather; the anti-Semitism his family and neighbors would endure in England; the loss of millions of Jews and Christians from his community; and the romance between his Jewish sister and her Christian boyfriend.

He would publish more books off the success of his memoirs, and kept writing until the last days of his life. Considering that The Invisible Wall wasn't published until he was 96 years old,

Harry Bernstein is a shining example of persistence. When he died in 2011, he was known as a successful author of four novels.

Principle:

Harry Bernstein's story is not just about being old and pursuing a dream; it's about finding inspiration, even if it's in the pain of loneliness. By writing his memoirs, he found a way to transform the agony of losing his precious wife into a passion.

Action:

No matter how old you are or how lonely your life may be, there's hope to change the defeat of pain into the success of achievement. The only true defeat is in admitting defeat.

It's never too late to write your novel, or shout from the highest mountain. If Harry Bernstein could do it at 93, you can too!

6

GEORGE BURNS

One of my favorite "success after 50" stories is George Burns (1896-1996). Although Burns, along with his wife and partner Gracie Allen, had enjoyed success in Vaudeville and in the early days of television, he hadn't done a movie in 35 years and was considered a washed-up actor.

But at the age of 79 he got the opportunity to play the lead role in Neil Simon's "The Sunshine Boys" with Walter Matthau after Jack Benny (one of his best friends who initially was to play the role) died unexpectedly.

The producers were very worried that Burn's age might cause him to forget his lines. So about a week before filming was to begin, all of the cast members were asked to come in for a screenplay reading.

When Burns arrived without the manuscript, the director and producers feared his memory was worse than they had imagined. But to their amazement, George had memorized not only his lines but those of the other cast members. His performance was so brilliant that he won an Oscar as Best Supporting Actor, thereby becoming the oldest winner in the history of the Academy Awards.

It's NEVER Too Late & You're NEVER Too Old

21

He went on to do ten more movies until he was almost 100, and endeared himself to a new generation of movie-goers.

Principle:

After experiencing early success, people may enter a period of stunted growth or failure. George Burns' success after 50 achievements can be summed up in one of his quotes: "The happiest people I know are the ones who are still working. The saddest are the ones who are retired."

Action:

You're on the verge of an exciting new beginning when you ignore your failures or lack of progress. It's never too late to rejuvenate an old career into a new one!

PAUL CÉZANNE

Though Paul Cézanne's (1839-1906) career began before he was 50, he would continue to mature as an artist until he died. Many of his greatest paintings occurred later in life rather than in his earlier years. And his French Post-Impressionist's works would lay the foundation for artistic explosion in the early 20th century.

Cézanne's close relationship with Pablo Picasso helped form his own style which is recognizable to anyone with a decent amount of knowledge of Post-Impressionism (a term coined by art critic Roger Fray in 1910 to describe the development of French art since Monet).

"Rideau, Cruchon et Compotier", "The Card Players", or "The Bathers" are among Cézanne's most notable works, all of which were painted after he had turned 50 (during perhaps his most influential years known as his "Final Period").

Cézanne became known as "the father of us all" to painters like Picasso and Matisse. But this might not have happened if he had been lived on the laurels of his early successes. Although by today's standards he had a short life, the masterpieces he painted turned the art world upside down.

Principle:

The experience of your youth can carry you throughout your life, as you never stop learning or honing your skills. Paul Cézanne is a perfect example of an artist who wanted to keep growing.

Many people are comfortable painting the same way their entire life (and for some people – like Grand Moses – it works). But Cézanne's skills grew because he was willing to adapt, change, and experiment. Even if you do something your entire life, you might not become proficient unless you're willing to push yourself to do difficult things.

Action:

Ask yourself if you're really practicing your skills and getting better, or merely repeating what you've always done. Do you feel like you've grown? Or have you stayed stagnant? There's an old saying, "If you're not growing, you're dying." So it's never too late have your skills become stronger and demand more from yourself!

8

RAYMOND CHANDLER

R aymond Chandler's (1888-1959) first novel, The Big Sleep, was published in 1939 when he was 51 years old.

Born in Nebraska, and eventually ending up in England, he was a reporter at a couple of newspapers including the Daily Express and Bristol Western Gazette.

Not considering himself much of a success, he borrowed money from his uncle and returned to America.

After his mother joined him in San Francisco, he studied book-keeping and worked at odd jobs like stringing tennis rackets and picking fruit, and eventually found steady work with a creamery.

Chandler fought in World War I with the Canadian Army, and after his release was hired by the Dabney Oil Syndicate Company (where he was eventually fired for womanizing, drinking, absenteeism, and threats of suicide).

At age 44, and without a way to make money, he started writing pulp fiction detective stories. His first novel, The Big Sleep, featured the detective Philip Marlowe who was formulated after the Perry Mason character, Erle Stanley Gardner.

He also had many of his early stories accepted by Black Mask, the same mystery magazine that had published Dashiell

Hammett's works. Chandler told his English publisher, Hamish Hamilton, "...it struck me that some of the writing was pretty forceful and honest, even though it had its crude aspect."

His success as a novelist led to a career in screenwriting, and Chandler was nominated for Oscars for best screenplay for "Double Indemnity" and "The Blue Dahlia."

Principle:

Raymond Chandler changed his life as a total misfit into a successful writing career. Sure, he still liked to drink (he even requested that he write one of his screenplays drunk). But in spite of his earlier screw-ups, there's no doubt he was determined to have a writing career, and a very successful one at that!

Action:

Don't let the turmoil of your personal life become an excuse for why your professional life can't be successful. Even if you haven't taken your life seriously until this point, you can leave your past behind. It's never too late to start a career before, during, or after the age of 50!

NIRAD C. CHAUDHURI

What if your greatest works came after 50, and didn't end until you were 100? This is exactly what happened to Nirad C. Chaudhuri (1897-1999), the Bengali-English writer and commentator who would eventually be knighted by Queen Elizabeth II.

Chaudhuri was born in Kishorenganj (at that time a part of Bengal, a region of British India, which is now known as Bangladesh). He contributed articles to newspapers and magazines in his early days as a clerk in the accounting department of the Indian Army. And later supported himself as a secretary to a major Indian political leader, and as a commentator for All India Radio.

However, his big breakthrough didn't come until his first major work, The Autobiography of an Unknown Indian, was published in 1951, which made him an instant hit at age 54. Chaudhuri's Thy Hand, Great Anarch! was published in 1987 when he was 90, and Three Horsemen of the New Apocalypse was published in 1997 when he was 100 years old.

He was awarded the Sahitya Akademi Award in 1975 for his biography on Max Müller called Scholar Extraordinary. In 1992 he was honored by Queen Elizabeth II with the title of Commander of Order of the British Empire. His 1965 novel, The Continent of Circe, earned him the Duff Cooper Memorial Award (the only Indian to be selected for the prize).

His writings, which resonated with a great deal of people worldwide, cut to the core of what was happening in India. Considering Chaudhuri began publishing after the age of 50, his remarkable achievements would be of interest to people at a later stage in their life wondering if they are still culturally relevant.

Principle:

People may spend years honing their skills with only modest success and recognition. But repeated effort can suddenly create a breakthrough moment and make them an overnight success.

Action:

What skill have you been passionately working at for years, but have yet to see them blossom? It's never too late to focus even more time and effort to creating your big breakthrough moment!

10

JULIA CHILD

Your recollection of Julia's Child's career might be her hit cooking show, "The French Chef." But what might be of interest is she didn't come to television until she was 50 years old in 1963.

Julia (née McWilliams) (1912-2004) was too tall to enlist in the WACs or the U.S Navy's WAVES, so she entered civil service as a typist at the OSS office in Washington, D.C. Because of her education, she was transferred into the intelligence division where she met her husband, Paul. They moved to Paris in 1948 where she attended the Le Cordon Bleu cooking school.

Having lived in Paris as an artist and poet, it was Paul who introduced his wife to fine cuisine. While writing a French cookbook with her friends Simonne Beck and Louisette Bertholle, and teaching American women how to cook, she experimented with recipes and translated many French recipes into English.

After the Childs returned to America, Alfred Knopf published Julia's Mastering the Art of French Cooking in 1961. Her promotional debut of the book on National Education Television was so widely receive by viewers that her cooking show, "The French Chef," was launched in 1963.

Julia's passion for cooking was born out of boredom in Paris while her husband was at work. But even more importantly, her desire to share her experiences and culinary skills with women around the world.

Principle:

Sometimes inspiration won't hit you until later in life, but that doesn't mean the success you reach after 50 can't be profound. Julia Child is a perfect example as her success ran for several decades once she learned how to dice onions and bone a duck.

Action:

Be willing to embrace your passions, no matter where they take you. Growing up, Julia Child wouldn't know her name would one day be synonymous with French cooking. But that's where her life took her because she was willing to master and follow her passion. If you're willing to embrace new things, it's never too late to journey into unknown adventures!

11

ADELA CHOQUET

Almost 40 years ago Adela Choquet decided to tag along with a friend to a South Florida yoga class. The 55-year-old Chilean had never heard of yoga before, and admitted she didn't like it at first. But since she was riding with her friend, she had no way home and decided to make the most of the three-hour class.

By the end of the session she had completely changed her mind, and yoga became her passion. "After three hours I said, 'I think I like this." And that being stranded was the best thing that could have happened to her.

Yoga involves particular postures and breathing techniques to increase the body's stamina, flexibility, remove stress, and increase physical and mental health. But in 2008 at the age of 92, a full Lotus position was no problem at all to Adela.

She says her biggest accomplishment has come from teaching yoga, which she's been doing since the 1970s. She still teaches a one-hour class three times a week to students over 55 (making her one of the oldest yoga teachers ever), and sees no reason to stop anytime soon. Her goal is to keep teaching until she turns 100!

Principle:

Though it didn't make her millions or a media celebrity, Adela nonetheless followed the path to a remarkable life. Instead of hanging out and waiting until her friend was done with the class, she said why not, which changed the course of her life. She allowed herself the time to literally warm up to a new experience, and then fell head over heels in love with her new passion.

Action:

Make the call today to find out about classes you've often thought about taking. Then get off the couch and go! It's never too late extend yourself into a new physicality, and it could just be the move(ment) of your lifetime!

WINSTON CHURCHILL

S ir Winston Leonard Spencer Churchill (1874-1965) is one of my all-time favorite heroes. Although his achievements are too vast to mention here, he is without a doubt one of the best examples of persistence the world has ever known.

With ongoing financial problems, defeated for office, washed up and exiled for ten years to the "political wilderness," he would eventually soar to achievements that would earn him the title of "Greatest Briton of All Time."

Born to aristocrats Lord and Lady Churchill, he started life with a speech impediment – a curiosity considering he would later become famous for his quick wit and rousing speeches. A life of military service suited him well, and he served in the British forces in Cuba, India, South Africa, and Sudan. After his military career he joined Parliament, winning a seat in the 1900 election. But he would later lose that position when the Conservatives were defeated in the 1929 election.

When the threat of Hitler loomed in the latter half of the 1930s, Churchill's concerns about the impending state of affairs in Europe grew more relevant. He vehemently criticized Prime Minister Neville Chamberlain, and advocated a hard line against

Germany. And it was his unrelenting, singular voice that won him the prime ministership once World War II broke out.

During the war he became famous for speeches such as "This was their finest hour," and "I have nothing to offer but blood, toil, tears, and sweat." When he said with unparalleled conviction, "We shall fight on the beaches, we shall fight on the landing grounds, we shall fight in the fields and in the streets, we shall fight in the hills, we shall never surrender," he had the entire country of England behind him. Winston Churchill would serve as Prime Minister into his late eighties.

Principle:

What better example of an indomitable spirit than the man who refused to let his country fall? Churchill's example of "grace under pressure" not only showed the world how to stand up to Hitler, but he inspired a country to defend itself no matter the cost. If it weren't for Sir Winston Churchill's resolve and fight against tyranny, it's entirely possible Europe would have collapsed and world history would have been forever altered.

Action:

If you remember only one lesson from Churchill's campaign to save England, it should be "Never give in. Never, never, never, never..." It's never too late to stand and fight for what's right!

13

JACK COVER

Jack Higson Cover (1920-2009) was highly educated. He earned a degree in nuclear physics from the University of Chicago while studying under the legendary Enrico Fermi.

After graduating, he served in World War II as an Army Air Force test pilot, and would eventually work as a scientist for companies as varied as North American Aviation, NASA's Apollo program, IBM, and Hughes Aircraft.

But the irony is his most famous contribution to the world of science would be one of his own inventions – the Taser.

Named for the TA.Ser (TASER), the electroshock device was finalized around 1974. Cover and Rick Smith founded Taser International in 1994, and the weapon has been used ever since by law enforcement to disarm and apprehend criminals with less risk of long-term physical harm.

Jack Cover was 50 years old when he formed Taser Systems, and had a lucrative career for many years thereafter.

Principle:

Your own business success might seem like a fantasy if you've been working for someone else your whole life. And by the time you reach the age of 50, you may feel like you have nothing new to offer the world. But Jack Cover proved you can design and develop a concept, and bring it to fruition.

You don't need to be an engineering expert or a rocket scientist. Take whatever talent you have (whether it's artistic, scientific, financial, or a love for inventions) and look for ways to solve people's problems or make their lives easier. For instance, Cover's TASER helps law enforcement protect themselves while doing less harm to people.

Even if nothing immediately comes to mind, you're probably more creative than you thought. So you need to work through obstacles and find that little nugget of inspiration.

Action:

Every time you encounter a challenge, ask yourself what solution could make it easier and write it down. For example, Art Fry was looking for a way to keep bookmarks from falling out of his hymn book. He had heard about a tacky adhesive that once applied could be easily removed, and thus was born the idea for Post-it Notes. It's never too late to invent something that could change people's lives!

14

RODNEY DANGERFIELD

Rodney Dangerfield (1921-2004) had been on the comedy circuit for a very long time. But it was a last-minute change on the Ed Sullivan Show in 1967 that started him on his path to success.

Dangerfield became an overnight hit and started appearing on other television programs like The Dean Martin Show and The Tonight Show in the 1970s. Then he started appearing in films such as Caddy Shack, Easy Money, and Back to School, which is quite a career achievement for the comedian nobody knew much about until he was 46 years old.

The theme of Dangerfield's act? His catchphrase, "I don't get no respect," that also became the title of his Grammy-winning comedy album. His famous one-liners became synonymous with his act as he continued performing into his 80s. The theme of 'no respect' is even on his gravestone: "Rodney Dangerfield...there goes the neighborhood."

Principle:

Rodney Dangerfield's comedic hook that he got no respect was congruent to his age and on-stage persona. And people responded to it immediately as soon as he started playing to bigger audiences.

Action:

Opportunity knocks in odd places and at odd times. You need to learn to roll with the punches, and use your misfortunes to inspire yourself to greater success. Rodney Dangerfield's most productive years were in the latter half of his life. So if you can recognize opportunities and capitalize on them as much as possible, it's never too late cement a long-lasting, positive reputation for yourself!

15

MELCHORA AQUINO DE RAMOS

Melchora Aquino (1812-1919) is another example of a woman who achieved fame later in life. Born in Balintawak, Philippines, although she never received formal education she was highly literate and a very talented singer. She married a village chief, and bore six children before being widowed.

During the Philippine Revolution, Melchora operated a store that would become a safe haven for sick and injured revolutionaries. But she didn't only provide medical attention and sustenance, she dispensed encouragement, motherly advice and prayers.

Melchora became known as "Tandang Sora" ("Elder Sora") because of her age when the revolution broke out in 1896 (she was 84). She is also known as the "Grand Woman of the Revolution," and the "Mother of Balintawak" for her heroic efforts on behalf of her people.

She was deported to Guam when the Spanish found out she was aiding revolutionaries. But was allowed to resume her life in the Philippines in 1898 after the United States defeated Spain during the Spanish-American War and took control of the islands. Melchora passed away at the age of 107.

Principle:

Melchora Aquino de Ramos became famous for her strong sense of community and loyalty. It's not so much that she fought the Spaniards or helped plan battles against them; it's that her dedication gave the Filipinos strength in their cause. Her love for her people earned their respect, and her generous spirit saved many lives.

Action:

Success doesn't live in a vacuum. It's often what you do in tandem with others that defines your legacy. This was certainly true in the case of Melchora Aquino who gave everything she had to her community.

The older you are, the more people can benefit from your wisdom and foresight. It's never too late to be of service for a cause, no matter how large or small!

16

MARJORIE STONEMAN DOUGLAS

P erhaps the most famous defender of the Florida Everglades, Marjorie Stoneman Douglas (1890-1998) didn't begin her life-defining work until she was in her fifties.

Marjorie was an only child, and grew up to go to Wellesley College in Massachusetts.

She met Kenneth Douglas in 1914, and was so impressed with his manners and his interest in her that they were married within a short three months.

When it turned out Douglas was a con artist (it was suspected he was already married) the marriage fell apart, and she joined her father's newspaper in 1915 (which would later be the Miami Herald).

Marjorie joined the Navy as a yeoman in World War I, then asked for a discharge to work in the Red Cross in Paris. Returning to the Miami Herald after the war with free reign to write what she wanted, she wrote about women's suffrage and was in opposition to Prohibition.

But it was her freelance work during the 1940s that eventually led to interest from a publisher who wanted her to contribute a story about the Miami River. The more she researched environmental issues in southern Florida, the more she wanted to write about the Everglades, especially when she found out they were in serious danger due to mismanagement.

At 57 she wrote a best-selling book – *The Everglades: River of Grass* – that continues be as important to conservationists and environmentalists as it did decades ago. In 1997 the Christian Science Monitor wrote, "Today her book is not only a classic of environmental literature, it also reads like a blueprint for what conservationists are hailing as the most extensive environmental restoration project ever undertaken anywhere in the world."

She also founded the Friends of the Everglades when she was 79 years old. Running the operation from her house, she grew the organization to some 3,000 members within a few years.

Although Marjorie stood all of 5'2" and weighed 100 pounds, she was a force to be reckoned with. She was well-respected for her knowledge on her subjects, and even critics applauded her authority on the Everglades. She stood her ground with bureaucrats and politicians, and chastised reporters who had never read her books.

In 1993 at the age of 103, President Bill Clinton awarded Marjorie Stoneman Douglas the Presidential Medal of Freedom, the highest honor ever given to a civilian.

Principle:

You're never too old to become passionate about a cause, and for Marjorie Douglas that was the Florida Everglades. She noticed that no one else seemed to be fighting for them, and figured she was as good as anyone to be its champion.

Action:

Your age may be an asset when championing a cause. It's easier to become a leader at an older age than it is at a younger age (with age comes wisdom, and with wisdom comes a good leader), so use your age to your advantage. It's never too late join the fight for something you believe in!

17

CLINT EASTWOOD

Of course the king of spaghetti Westerns isn't a late-bloomer. But considering how hard it can be to stay relevant in Hollywood, Clint Eastwood's an exemplary example of what you can do to reinvent yourself and keep yourself relevant until your advanced years.

Eastwood rose to fame for his portrayal of grizzly Western characters in movies like "The Good, the Bad, and the Ugly" (1966). In fact, he had done so well with characters like the Man With No Name (a stock character in Western films) and Dirty Harry, that he easily could have retired as a Hollywood legend if he was content to ride into the sunset on his fame.

But Eastwood was too ambitious to retire. Instead, he started directing movies in the mid-1970s (like "The Outlaw Josey Wales" in which he starred and directed). Then he started making more sophisticated movies like "Unforgiven," which earned him an Oscar for Best Director. And "Mystic River," an ambitious World War II project that kept him occupied him in the mid-2000s. Then came "Invictus," "Gran Torino," "Hereafter," and "J. Edgar."

In 2004, Clint Eastwood was the oldest director to win the Academy Award for "Million Dollar Baby" (along with Hilary

Based on the original photo by Fanny Bouton.

Swank who won the award for Best Actress). He was 74 when he accepted his first Oscar (he won two for "Million Dollar Baby," and two for "Unforgiven" in 2009).

Principle:

As I wrote earlier, Clint Eastwood certainly wasn't a late bloomer. But after he reinvented himself via his directing career, his Hollywood legacy would be drastically different than if he had retired and quit filmmaking.

Action:

Staying relevant in what is usually considered a young man's game in Hollywood is almost impossible, but Eastwood succeeded by acknowledging his limitations. Since he's no longer a young action star, he plays to his current strengths which is directing and acting. It's never too late play to your strengths, and keep yourself active, vital, and a participant in your life!

18

CHRIS GARDNER

Chris Gardner's story began with a violent, challenging childhood. Born in 1954 he was raised in abject poverty, domestic violence, alcoholism, sexual abuse, and illiteracy.

He joined the Navy out of high school, and after his discharge he moved to San Francisco where he got jobs in medical research supplies. The jobs weren't well-paying, however, and when he became a single father he knew he had to find something more lucrative.

Gardner was always good at math, and his interest in finance landed him an intern stockbroker's job. But mistakes from his days selling medical research supplies landed him in deep debt and garnishment by the IRS. For an entire year Gardner and his son were homeless. They slept in flophouses, motels, parks, airports, on public transport and even in a locked bathroom at a BART station. Days without meals were commonplace.

Wrangling his way into Dean Witter as a trainee, he showed up to work early every day and made cold calls to prospective clients. In 1982, Gardner's perseverance paid off when he passed his licensing exam and became a full-time employee. This success led him to eventually starting Gardner Rich & Co. in his apartment. Today he is a very wealthy entrepreneur, philanthropist, motivational speaker, and benefactor for the homeless.

At age 52 Gardner felt his struggles could be an inspiration to others, so he published his memoirs called The Pursuit of Happyness. In 2006, his best-selling novel was made into a movie (starring Will Smith who was nominated for an Academy Award). He later stated the main reason for writing his autobiography was to show people that struggles in childhood don't have to define them as an adult.

Principle:

Chris Gardner's success isn't measured in dollars and cents, but in a change in identity. He never knew his father, and was in foster homes a good portion of his childhood. He pledged that even in the most dire of circumstances he would never be absent from his son (there were times during their homelessness when he had to fight to keep custody). Gardner's change in finances was a reflection of the inner changes shaped by his circumstances.

Action:

If you're over 50 and still living in the past, it's time to release bad memories and create new ones. If you don't know where to start, you need to ask yourself how you define success. Chris Gardner proved to the world that nothing and no one was going to stop him from getting work in order to take care of his son. It's never too late to prove you've got what it takes!

19

MILLIE GARFIELD

When she was 78 years old, and thanks to her son Steve's encouragement, Millie Garfield took up blogging on the Internet.

Describing herself growing up as a "quiet little girl," she is considered one of the Internet's oldest bloggers (aka: Elderbloggers), and is still going strong with a very loyal global audience.

Her blog located at http://mymomsblog.blogspot.com/ (her video postings can also be found at http://www.urlesque. com/2010/01/19/millie-garfield/) keeps readers in the loop as to the goings-on of her life.

In fact, so many people are interested in Millie that they're following her blog just to keep tabs on her. She also covers things like selling her condo, what she's doing for Mother's Day, and her opinions on the latest movies.

Millie's success isn't just about building a popular blog, but about connecting with people. Many comments have been about how sharp and young Millie has been able to keep herself over the years. And her blogging success has been discussed by ABC, the Wall Street Journal, and the Washington Post.

Principle:

New technology can be intimidating as we get older, but if we're willing to embrace it we may find the most rewarding work of our life. Millie Garfield exemplifies that no matter how old you are, people will follow you if you've got an interesting voice and have something worth saying.

Action:

If blogging doesn't trip your trigger, look for other ways to express yourself. As Millie says, the thinking that's involved helps keep you younger. It's never too late have a voice and use it!

20

VÁCLAV HAVEL

The first president of the Czech Republic, Václav Havel's story was one of political opposition that eventually led to victory and leadership of his native country.

Born in Prague in 1936, Havel grew up in a relatively affluent and intelligent family – one that was certainly well-tuned to the political events around his early life that coincided with the rise and fall of the Nazi regime in Germany.

After he finish Czech military service, Havel turned to the theater to express himself and debuted a full-length play he had written in 1963. One of his plays even gained popularity in the United States, showing that Havel also had international appeal.

After the Communists banned his work from theaters, Havel became a political dissident and joined the resistance during the invasion of Czechoslovakia in the 1960s. He also became known for his essays in support of the movement, which helped cement his reputation as a local hero and a passionate fighter for Czech independence.

At age 53, Havel became the leader of the Civic Forum that organized against the Communist government. After they were driven from office, he became president of Czechoslovakia in

1989. Later, when the republic split from Slovakia, Havel became the first president of the Czech Republic in 1993. By the time of his death in 2011, he had become chairman of the New York-Based Human Rights Foundation, founder of the VIZE 97 Foundation, and principal organizer of the Forum global conference.

Principle:

When Václav Havel's passion of writing was taken away from him, he found other ways to express himself and make an impact. He threw himself into his work in political resistance as he had during his days as a playwright.

Action:

Instead of fretting over a passion that's no longer plausible due to changing circumstances, find another one you can pour your energy into. By now, you should realize it's never too late to realize your destiny!

21

ALFRED HITCHCOCK

An icon in the mystery film genre, Alfred Hitchcock (1899-1980) became so entrenched in making movies that his work spanned decades.

But it wasn't until he turned 50 that he directed "Strangers on a Train" (1951); "Dial M For Murder" (1954); "Rear Window" (1954); "The Man Who Knew Too Much" (1956); "Vertigo" (1958); "North by Northwest" (1959); "Psycho" (1960); and "The Birds" (1963).

Born in England, his journey took him from being an engineering draftsman, advertising designer, and as a cadet in the military Royal Engineers. It was during his time at Henley's as a designer that he started writing stories that would eventually end up as films.

He ended up in Germany where he would learn to direct, and moved to Hollywood with his wife, Alma, in 1939 after David O. Selznick signed him to a seven-year contract. Selznick knew a good thing when he saw all the favorable reviews on Hitchcock in the U.K. and Germany.

In essence, the Hitchcock of those earlier films was not the Hitchcock fans came to know after he moved to the U.S. But as

a seasoned director in his 50s and 60s going through a career renaissance. He even remade some of his earlier movies (i.e., the 1934 "The Man Who Knew Too Much" he recast in 1956 with James Stewart and Doris Day).

There are a number of reasons Hitchcock had become so successful by this point. First, he had already earned a reputation as a sterling filmmaker. Second, he had grown familiar with a number of famous actors including Cary Grant, Jimmy Stewart, and Grace Kelly. And third, he had honed his personal style to a level not previously seen in film. In essence it was Hitchcock's life experience that gave filmgoers their greatest thrills.

Principle:

Alfred Hitchcock built on his previous success as a filmmaker to become even more successful after the age of 50. By industry standards, Steven Spielberg was quite young when he directed "Jaws", "Raiders of the Lost Ark," and "E.T.: The Extraterrestrial." But Hitchcock's movie-making legacy came after he turned 50, which is how fans of his thrillers such as "Vertigo" (1958) and "Marnie" (1964) remember him.

Action:

Instead of using your age as an excuse not to follow your dream, build on your experience and hone your style. It's never too late to be in your director's chair, and the creator of your own life's movie!

22

EDMOND HOYLE

There are spades, diamonds, clubs, hearts and jokers in a deck of cards. But when you see a card that explains the rules of a particular game, you mostly likely have Edmond Hoyle to thank for it.

Hoyle (1672-1769) became best known for writing the rules and plays of card games. In fact, he became such an authority that the phrase "according to Hoyle" became a staple in the English language when he wrote primarily about the game of whist, and was so proficient that he would tutor high-society players. He turned his notes into a pamphlet, A Short Treatise on the Game of Whist, which eventually became one of the foremost card game manuscripts ever published.

But Hoyle didn't publish the pamphlet until he was 70 years old (imagine how old that would be in the 18th century when the average life expectancy was 40 years). He would go on to write more about games, including brag, probability theory, backgammon, and chess. Although Edmond Hoyle died before poker was invented, he is nonetheless in the Poker Hall of Fame.

Principle:

In his classic work, Lead the Field, Earl Nightingale said that in "five years or less you can become a true expert in your field. And it's the experts who write their own tickets in life." Thanks to modern technology that time has shrunk to a year or less to become a national expert. That's right, a year or less!

I went from obscurity to becoming an internationally known expert in personal developing and goal-setting in about 18 months. And that was after I was 50 years old! My first speaking gig commanded $7,500 plus expenses. In fact, a little over an hour's worth of speaking I made half as much money as I had made the entire year of 1997!

Older people in many cultures and religious sects are highly revered for their knowledge. Whether you realize it or not you are an expert in many areas, no matter how small or large (who would have thought that Hoyle could become wealthy and famous just by writing about card playing!).

Action:

Make a list of things you know a lot about. It could be deck building, training dogs, kite flying, recipes or cooking – everyone is an expert on something. Focus on one area where you'd like to position yourself as an expert. For Hoyle, it was the game of whist. For Colonel Sanders, it was fried chicken. For me it was as a motivational speaker. Hopefully by these examples you can see that expertise in most any field can be worth a great deal of fame and fortune, and that it's never too late to start!

23

SISTER MARION IRVINE

The story of Sister Marion Irvine is not only about someone who achieved great success late in life, but was able to overcome stereotypes about who she was in order to do what she loved.

By 1976 when she was 47 years old, this Roman Catholic nun was smoking two packs of cigarettes per day and was severely out of shape.

Her niece suggested that she try jogging (because as she said she "had a lot of pent-up energy that wasn't being used"), so she bought running shoes and shorts and started running every day.

Not only was Sister Marion the supervisor of several Dominican schools, but she turned heads when running in the rain (at that time a "running nun" was unheard of).

In 1981 at the age of 51, she won the veteran female division of the Boston Marathon. In 1983, at the California International Marathon she completed the race in 2 hours, 51 minutes and 1 second, breaking the women's over-50 marathon record by more than 8 minutes which qualified her to compete in the 1984 Olympic trials. This made Sister Marion the oldest person ever to qualify for the Olympic Trials.

After winning other record-breaking events, she was inducted into the RRCA Hall of Fame in 1994, having retired in 1993 because she knew she didn't have the strength to continue running. Sadly, due to stenosis (a degenerative condition of the spinal discs) she is unable to run even for exercise, but walks and hikes whenever she can.

Principle:

If a nun over the age of 50 can run, why can't you? Sister Marion Irvine's story should inspire you by proving you don't have to be limited by your vocation or your age.

Action:

Go for a run, even if it turns a few heads. It's never too late to be as physically active as your body allows, and having goals like the Olympics is not unrealistic!

24

RAY KROC

There aren't many business success stories like that of Ray Kroc, even if he wasn't the founder of the McDonald's restaurant franchise.

That honor belonged to Dick and Mac McDonald who placed an order for multi-mixers for milkshakes from the company Kroc represented.

Intrigued by why a restaurant would need that many mixers, Kroc investigated their business model and loved their principals. "I said, 'that's for me,'" he later recalled.

Although it was the McDonald brothers who pioneered the original restaurant concept, it was Kroc who would think of franchising McDonald's on a much grander scale. After debating the brothers about how much it should be expanded, Kroc bought the company in 1961 for over $2 million when he was 59 years old.

People took to franchising the restaurant in a way that was unprecedented. Today, McDonald's is one of the world's largest corporations, and next to Coca-Cola is one of the most recognized brands.

Kroc's story is even more remarkable when you consider he became interested in McDonald's simply because of an order for milkshake makers. But the smell of success became so overwhelming that he had no choice but to follow it.

Principle:

You don't have to come up with an idea to realize where there's money to be made. Ray Kroc made McDonald's famous worldwide because knew an opportunity when he saw it, and was willing to take action because of his belief in the business model.

Action:

Move in swiftly when you smell an opportunity, and don't be afraid to approach people you don't know. Ray Kroc did travel from Illinois to California, where it turned out he had found the opportunity of a lifetime. Imagine if he had thought, I'm too old to start something on a whim.

The tools of success is your imagination, an eye for opportunity, a leap of faith, and galvanizing into action. It's never too late to grab that brass ring!

25

ABRAHAM LINCOLN

As the 16th President of the United States, Abraham Lincoln (1809-1865) is widely known because of what he accomplished late in life. But many people don't know about the failure and pain that went into his journey toward success.

Self-educated, Abraham Lincoln achieved a certain amount of success before his presidency. He became a country lawyer, Whig party leader, and Illinois State legislator, and served one term as a member of the House of Representatives. But all of these were just stepping stones to his life as president of the United States.

It was through the nomination of a new political party (Republicans) where Lincoln would ultimately win the presidency, rise to national prominence, lead the Union against the Confederacy in the Civil War, and abolish slavery.

When he took office – only his second federal office after his short stint in Congress – he was over 50 years old. He would earn re-election to the presidency, but his plans for Reconstruction of the South would unfortunately be left to his replacements as he was assassinated in 1865 by John Wilkes Booth.

Many conversations have occurred about what Lincoln would have accomplished had he lived longer. But the son of Thomas

and Nancy Lincoln, and the husband of Mary Todd Lincoln, managed to overcome his adversities and live life large.

Principle:

Abraham Lincoln didn't have an easy life. Most people know the story of being born in a one-room log cabin. His mother died when he was very young, and his family suffered great hardships. The nation he held together during the war years split in half (you can see the toll it took in photographs taken during his term in office). He lived through the death of two of his sons, and his wife Mary would be committed to a mental asylum (albeit on a temporary basis). But Lincoln became famous for being steadfast in his leadership, and never giving in to naysayers.

Action:

While your greatest successes might come after 50, it's important to remember your greatest burdens might come then as well. Like Lincoln, you can overcome adversity if you believe in what you're fighting for. It's never too late to stand up for your principles!

26

FRANNY MARTIN

Franny Martin had a 30-year corporate marketing career working for a number of companies (including Burger King, McDonald's and Domino's Pizza). Then one day she had the revelation that this wasn't what she wanted to be doing. She was 56 years old when she was hit by the lightning bolt epiphany that would change her life forever.

Franny's husband had already told her how great her cookies were. "I was ready to do something different, and I always loved baking, so I decided to open a cookie business," said Martin, who started testing cookie recipes on friends.

As her reputation as a baker grew, she personally delivered the dozen different kinds cookies within a 20-mile radius.

When customers started asking if she would ship her cookies, Martin knew she was on to something big and created her company, Cookies on Call. Today they produce 42 types of cookies, and ship to 48 states and almost a dozen countries including China, England, Israel, Saudi Arabia, France and Switzerland.

Franny Martin's advice for mid-life entrepreneurs? "Do what you love and the money will follow."

Principle:

Your change doesn't have to be gradual. Like Franny Martin, one day you could have an epiphany that will change the direction of your life.

Of course, taking a risk can be scary. Even if you don't have the advantage of savings and/or a spouse to lean on, you can start from scratch. And nobody started from "scratch" quite like Franny Martin who learned how to deliver her cookies before she even figured out how to ship them. Hundreds of thousands of businesses have been started by "solo-preneurs," and there are many different ways of finding seed money and partners to get your business started.

Action:

Listen to the call from within and pay attention at it's telling you your purpose. You don't have to quit your job today, but you should make a decision about where you want to go and take the steps to get there. It's never too late to become the next Famous Amos or Franny Martin!

LEE MARTIN

I f an 88-year-old blogger sounds old, wait till you hear about Lee Martin who was featured in a Chicago Tribune article in 2006, calling him "probably the oldest bartender in Chicago." He was 94 years old at the time.

The former Missouri farm boy recalled how he came to Chicago in 1945 after spending his young adulthood employed by the federal government in Washington, D.C., and Crown Point, Indiana.

Martin spent most of his life working in banking and at an interior-decorating company. But as he neared retirement, a chance conversation with the owner of a bar he frequented (Tischer's, which was later renamed to Richard's) led to a career as a bartender.

Most patrons have no idea of Martin's age. Long accustomed to questions about his longevity, the never-married Martin answers, "Drinking booze and chasing young women, because I could never catch 'em."

Sadly, Guinness World Records doesn't have a category for the World's Oldest Bartender. But even without the title, Martin has been an institution among the bar's patrons who enjoyed his folksy, relaxed style, and marvel at his youthful appearance.

Principle:

Reaching the retirement age of 65 doesn't mean you have to retire from your life altogether, as you can reinvent yourself and have your dream career.

Action:

Pick the brains of people older than you who began their second (or third) professions to find out what they did to get started. It's never too late to reinvent and rejuvenate your life, and do something you've always wanted to do!

FRANK McCOURT

Since I've mentioned successful, older authors, I can't skip the shining example of Frank McCourt (1930-2009), a Pulitzer Prize-winning author whose first book, Angela's Ashes, was published when he was 66.

McCourt was born in New York to Irish parents. They eventually moved back to Ireland during the Great Depression where they lived in horrible poverty (which he writes about in Angela's Ashes, with McCourt's father drinking away the family money and both parents unable to find very high-paying work).

His twin siblings, Oliver and Eugene, died in childhood, and he nearly died during a bout of typhoid fever at the age of 11.

McCourt quit school at age 13, and took on many jobs and petty crime to support himself and his family. He was a post office worker, served in the Korean War at age 19, and eventually taught creative writing in the New York public school system for 27 years.

It wasn't until age 66 when he published his memoir, Angela's Ashes, which earned McCourt fame, global notoriety, and a Pulitzer Prize for Biography.

In his first novel, he recounts stories from his childhood that shaped him into the man he eventually became. His second and third books ('Tis, follow-up to Angela's Ashes, and Teacher Man, about his time in the school system) were also acclaimed successes.

Although Frank McCourt died at the age of 78, his name lives on with the Frank McCourt High School of Writing, Journalism, and Literature in New York City.

Principle:

Frank McCourt's upbringing was no doubt a tough one. But his ability to write a Pulitzer Prize winner is testimony to what can be achieved without having literary training (and just because a person isn't published doesn't mean they're not a writer). McCourt taught writing, was encouraged by his students to write because he was so brilliant at it, and with determination he finally published his own works. It was his life's experiences that enabled to bring his memoirs into light, and brought success to him in his later years.

Action:

Frank McCourt was well into retirement age when he first found fame and notoriety. Retirement or transitioning out of a career doesn't have to be an end to your story. In fact, it's never too late start a new chapter in your life. Yes, retirement can provide plenty of time to work on projects and hobbies. But if you're not using your time constructively, you have no one to blame but yourself.

TAIKICHIRO MORI

At the time of his father's death, Taikichiro Mori (1904-1993) was successful as the head of the School of Commerce at Yokohama City University. Although that's no small feat, Mori's later achievements would dwarf his previous four decades of work.

Not only did he quit his job at the age of 55 to become a real estate mogul, he helped rebuild Tokyo into the sprawling metropolis it is today. And by the 1990s he had become the world's wealthiest man.

When Taikichiro Mori died, his company controlled some 83 buildings in Tokyo's center, which is still considered one of the most exclusive places in the world to own property. His net worth was considered around $13 billion.

Principle:

At the time of his transition from professor to entrepreneur, Taikichiro Mori was an academic with no experience in real estate or development. Much of his success came as a result of his concern about the people who would be most impacted by his developments. His first investments were in areas he remembered from childhood that had fallen on hard times.

Action:

Don't let your current situation and age prevent you from following your dream. Sometimes achieving success means you might have to do some scary things. Mori developed a plan and embraced his fears, and proved that there is no limit to success. Your fears or your age shouldn't prevent you from taking action as it's never too late to start!

GRANDMA MOSES

Anna Mary Robertson Moses (aka: "Grandma" Moses, 1860-1961) got a late start as a renowned folk artist. For the majority of her life, she and her husband raised a family of 10 children (five would die in infancy) first on a farm in Virginia, then in Eagle Bridge, New York.

During those years she showed an inclination toward creativity – not as a painter but as an embroiderer. When her arthritis made it difficult to hold a needle (and the lack of practicality of embroidering something that was quickly destroyed by moths), she created one of her first paintings as a Christmas gift for the postman, noting "it was easier to make than to bake a cake over a hot stove."

She was 76 years old when she started painting for gifts, and selling them for a few dollars. But it wasn't until much later when Grandma Moses would become known for her familiar folk style.

New York art collector, Louis J. Caldor, saw some of her paintings at a local drug store. Considering them a bargain at between $3.00 and $5.00, he bought them all and traveled to her home to buy even more. When her paintings debuted at the Museum of

Modern Art just a year later, Moses became an overnight sensation.

By the end of her life, she had painted over 1,600 canvasses. And in 2006 "Sugaring Off" sold for a cool $1.2 million. Not bad for a little old lady with a penchant for hobby art.

Principle:

Despite feeling the pangs of age, Grandma Moses expressed herself through a hobby where she had no formal training. If one door closes (her embroidery), simply open the next one (her painting).

Action:

Don't fret if you can't pursue something you've mastered in the past. You should be willing to use your talents in similar and equally effective ways. It's never too late to express your talents (in this case artistic creativity)!

31

NOLA OCHS

M any people may not have heard of Nola Ochs (née Hill). But graduating from Fort Hays State University in Kansas at the age of 95 put her in the Guinness Book of World Records as the world's oldest college graduate. On that exciting day, she received her degree in general studies with an emphasis in history alongside her 21-year-old granddaughter, Alexandra.

Nola was born in 1911 and took her first college class from FHSU in 1930 when the university was originally called Kansas State College.

She and her husband, Vernon, raised four sons (who have given her 13 grandchildren and 15 great-grandchildren) on the family farm. She went to the Dodge City Community College after Vernon died in 1972. Learning she was only 30 hours shy of a bachelor's degree, she moved to Hays to finish her degree, and was given her diploma in 2007 by Kansas Governor Kathleen Sebelius.

Then after a nine-day cruise as a guest lecturer, and taking time to help with the family wheat harvest, Nola pursued her master's in liberal studies Fort Hays State University. And on May

15, 2010, she became the oldest recipient of a master's degree at age 98.

As of her 100th birthday in November 2011, Nola Ochs was an M.A Student at FHSU and a Graduate Teaching Assistant.

Principle:

The best part of this story is Nola Och's ambition to continue her education because she wanted to, and nothing or no one was going to stop her.

If you've ever felt like an old person in a young person's game, imagine how she felt taking classes alongside 19 and 20-year-olds. But to Nola, completing a college degree for her own satisfaction was much more important than how people looked at her. Her success is a lesson of how far resolution and determination can take you in life.

Action:

Even in your twilight years you can take small steps that can lead to a very satisfying achievement. No matter how old you are and or how small the accomplishment may seem, it's never too late to take action toward a dream!

32

CLARA PELLER

If you remember Wendy's 1983 "Where's the Beef?" campaign, you'll remember spunky Clara Peller (1902-1987).

Raising two children as a single mother, she made a living for 35 years as a manicurist. That alone would have satisfied many women.

But when this tiny senior (who could barely see over the top of a steering wheel) caught the attention of the Dancer Fitzgerald ad agency that had seen her in an ad for a barbershop, her life would no longer be the same.

It was at the "young" age of 81 when Clara appeared in the Wendy's ad that would make her famous, and help the financially struggling franchise. If it wasn't her sharpness of spirit and her raspy voice, she might not have ever been noticed. But she made such an impact that even Walter Mondale used "Where's the beef?" as a slogan for his presidential campaign in 1984.

Clara made the most of her short-lived fame. She appeared on Saturday Night Live (a crowning honor), in a couple movies that played off her slogan, and on Wrestlemania. She benefitted from products using her iconic face such as coffee mugs, beach towels, t-shirts, a board game, and even a doll.

But she was fired by Wendy's when she appeared in a Prego commercial holding a jar of sauce and exclaiming, "I found it! I really found it!" Fireball Clara Peller passed away at age 85 in her native Chicago.

Principle:

Clara loved her life, and kept a youthful spirit about all her projects. After all, if she hadn't put her heart and soul into the barbershop ad, she might not have been discovered by Dancer Fitzgerald. She was noticed because she was an "outlier" (someone who stands out in spite of their advanced age), and because she was sassy. What you saw what was you got.

Action:

Stop thinking you need to save yourself for one major project. If you give yourself fully to everything you tackle – no matter how large or small – you're bound to be noticed. Even if you're not in a national ad campaign like Clara, your purpose is to make an impact during your time on earth. Live each day with enthusiasm, and good things will happen. It's never too late to stand out from the crowd and shout "Where's MY beef?"!

33

IRENE WELLS PENNINGTON

Claude B. "Doc" Pennington was a rich oilman who lived in Louisiana. When he started to lose his mental capacities, it was questionable as to whether or not he still had the capacity to run his business.

Enter his wife Irene. Though somewhat older than Doc, she had him declared mentally incompetent to protect the family estate, and took over the business and their finances. At that time, their wealth was estimated to be somewhere in the ballpark of $600 million.

The switch in roles surprised many people. Irene was older than her husband, so how could she have greater mental capacity than him? They also felt she didn't need to step up to the plate in the way she did. After all, it was her husband who had become a wealthy oilman and gave her the life she had been leading.

But what surprised people even more was that she efficiently straightened out her husband's affairs. She did an effective job at managing the finances, hiring and firing managers, and eventually setting up the estate to prepare for her own death.

Today, the Pennington family owns a great deal of land in southern Louisiana, and they have Irene's bold and decisive moves to thank for it.

Principle:

It was Irene's ability to sniff out the necessary actions that made her relevant. She knew what needed to be done, and knew that nobody was about to do it for her. She legally took charge of the company and made sure that she, her husband, and her family were taken care of. Irene Pennington earned notoriety for doing what needed to be done when she easily could have waited for old age to put her in a nursing home.

Action:

Everyone ages differently, and their health can't be compared other people simply because they are at a certain age. No matter how old you are, if you're mentally competent you're still required to take action in certain circumstances. Responsibility for your finances doesn't end simply because you're old; it ends when you no longer have the capacity to handle them yourself.

Doc Pennington had to give up his responsibilities because he was losing his mental capacity. His wife, Irene, stepped in and did what it took to ensure the family retained its financial stability. So matter how old you are, it's never too late step up to the plate!

34

A. C. BHAKTIVEDANTA SWAMI PRABHUPADA

T hough his name might be difficult to remember, the impact he had on the world is unforgettable.

Born in 1896 and dying in 1997, it was around 1966 when the Swami would make his mark on Western culture.

After he sailed to the United States in 1965 (at this point he was 71 years old), he founded the International Society for Krishna Consciousness (ISKCON) in New York City, which became more widely known as Hare Krishna (the Swami was adamant about changing the name as Krishna includes all other forms and concepts of God.)

During this time a handful of devotees traveled to London where they came in contact with the Beatles. Spiritually-minded George Harrison met with Bhaktivedanta, and would become an ardent follower of the Swami.

The last ten years of his life were focused on promoting global awareness of the Krishna consciousness. Not only did Bhaktivedanta travel the world during his later years, he authored a number of books (some claim more than 80.)

Principle:

Some people think that "old age" means they're supposed to slow down (the actual definition of retirement is "withdrawal from one's position or occupation or from active working life.") But that's ridiculous, as you can adapt your skills to suit your body. The only limitation is your desire and passion for your cause.

Bhaktivedanta reportedly went around the world 14 times during his twilight years. Hopefully you can see that age is more how you feel about yourself than how long you've been on earth.

Action:

A deep, passionate cause will move you to greater heights than simply "trying a new hobby." You may feel inspired to write a series of books on bullying, make towers out of paper clips for a children's organization, run a marathon to benefit diabetes, or create a spiritual following. It's never too late to find the passion that will fuel your success.

35

RONALD REAGAN

However a person feels about the politics of Ronald Reagan (1911-2004), it's hard to deny his greatest achievements came after the age of 50. In 1981, he became the oldest man to be elected the presidency at the age of 69.

Reagan was already famous as an actor when he played George Gipp in the movie "Knute Rockne, All American" (1940), which would earn him his nickname, "the Gipper." However, being one of the brightest stars in Hollywood was not what ultimately defined his fame and reputation.

Showing a natural instinct for leadership led to being elected to the Screen Actors Guild board of directors in 1941, and later its president. He eventually became a prominent Republican even before being elected to office, impressing party bigwigs with his 1964 speech "A Time for Choosing."

When movie mogul Jack Warner heard about Reagan running for governor of California, he supposedly said, "No, no. Jimmy Stewart for governor. Ronald Reagan for best friend." After serving eight years as governor, Reagan ran for president in 1976 but was beaten by incumbent Gerald Ford.

He was sworn into office as president in 1981 after he beat then-incumbent, President Jimmy Carter. Reagan would go on to win a second election, and at the end of his political career he would see his vice president, George H.W. Bush, be elected as 41st president.

Principle:

Though Ronald Reagan was rich, famous, and successful before 50, it was his life-defining turn into politics after 50 that would ultimately cement his name in history. No matter how successful you've been at making a name for yourself in one field (such as acting), there's no reason you can't play on a bigger stage (such as politics).

Action:

What "bigger stage" can you identify that's been calling to you? What have you always longed to do, but felt you're stuck in your current career or have "stage fright"? What can you do today to stick all ten toes in the water?

People change, they grow, they learn, they experience. And through all of that they become different people with different desires. So it's never too late switch careers and be all that you can be!

36

ORVILLE REDENBACHER

Orville Redenbacher (1907-1995) was working with corn long before he became the famous face of popcorn. In many ways his career mirrors that of Colonel Sanders, because it wasn't until later in life that Redenbacher became a national brand icon.

Growing up in Indiana Redenbacher earned a lot of money in the fertilizer industry, but that wasn't where he was destined to earn his fame. He and his partner Charlie Bowman bought a seed corn plant in the 1950s where they tirelessly worked to find the right kind of popping corn. Apparently they went through tens of thousands of trial and errors, and eventually found the right formula.

The Redenbacher popcorn operation was launched in 1970 when Orville was over the age of 60. Their extensive marketing programs succeeded, and their popcorn became a national brand.

Though he eventually sold the business (just as Harland Sanders had), he remained the face of the brand. Today, the Orville Redenbacher popcorn is a staple in American homes.

Principle:

Many of Redenbacher's business principles were the same as Harland Sanders. But when you consider what Orville and Charlie went through in order to find popping corn worthy of their customers' money, you get an idea of the dedication Redenbacher brought to his company.

Action:

At an age when many people are planning for retirement, Orville Redenbacher was still trying to find the perfect popcorn. Have you been thinking about giving up and going out to pasture? Well, it's never too to try out those ideas you've had for an invention or product!

37

GARY RUSSO

Fifty-year-old Gary Russo started August, 2011 as a New York ironworker, Local 40, working on the 2ndAvenue subway. By the end of the month, videos of him singing Sinatra songs during his lunch hour had been seen by millions, and he suddenly had a new career ahead of him.

Russo always had a desire to sing, but had limited it to karaoke, singing in the shower, his car, and in front of a mirror. Encouraged by a friend, he decided to set up his karaoke machine just outside the subway construction site.

Earning the nickname "Second Avenue Sinatra," he's been featured on numerous national and international shows including ABC's Good Morning America, NBC's Nightly News with Brian William, and Access Hollywood. Inside Edition filmed his debut at the famed Blue Note Jazz Club.

His book, Don't Die with Your Song Unsung (2011), is about transforming your life so you can achieve success by doing what you love. (He's also produced CDs.)

Principle:

Many people have a secret dream to perform – be it singing, acting, juggling, dancing, sword swallowing, magic – whatever it may be. And the truth is millions of people are as talented as people who achieve stardom.

But your voice will never be heard, and your magic tricks will never be seen if you don't take steps to bring that dream to life, regardless of how old you are. Even something as simple (and some would say silly) as singing karaoke for strangers can be your magic wand to a new life.

Action:

You've been putting your dream off long enough. Dust it off, and find a way to put yourself in front of an audience, no matter how small or large. With the right attitude, enthusiasm and persistence, you might be pleasantly surprised by the reception.

As Gary Russo says, "I have always felt there was a true artist hidden inside of me. Don't be afraid to share your talent with the world. It's never too late to follow your heart. You never know what life has in store for you." Did you get that? IT'S NEVER TOO LATE!

HARLAND DAVID "COLONEL" SANDERS

I f you read the Introduction, you already know a bit about the life of Colonel Sanders. But let's "zoom out" a bit and provide some further context for his amazing life.

Saying the Colonel was a complete failure until the age of 50 – and continued until he began his life's work at the age of 65 – is a bit of an exaggeration. Indeed, Sanders had a failed restaurant, but not until after some years of noteworthy success.

Harland Sanders was made an honorary "colonel" of Kentucky in 1935, decades ahead of when he became famous for his fried chicken. He received the title because his restaurant – noteworthy because of its "secret" recipe – had become a local legend.

If the Food Network had existed back in Colonel Sanders' earlier days, it's possible his restaurant would have been on TV before his franchise. In fact, food critic Duncan Hines put it in his "Adventures in Good Eating" guide, which happened in the 1930s (years before the Colonel's efforts in branding Kentucky Fried Chicken in the '50s and '60s).

Even though the Colonel had established himself as a local legend (or more accurately, "eccentric"), it would be his tenacity

after the age of 65 that would make him famous, and make him an icon of American ingenuity and success.

Principle:

Even if you're accomplished before the age of 50, there is no reason you can't be even more accomplished after 50. At 65, Sanders could have been quite content with his local legend status and retire, albeit with a social security check as his only source of income. But when the interstate was built and he had to close his restaurant, fate stepped in and he redirected his life.

Action:

Even with everything you've achieved, ask yourself if there's something you've always wanted to achieve or create. Then decide whether or not that dream might be something worth pursuing. It's never too late to dust of a favorite recipe, pull out the paint box from the closet, or take voice lessons. If one tiny little recipe for crispy chicken made the Colonel his fortune, imagine what you're passionate about can do for you!

39

ERNESTINE SHEPHERD

"Age is nothing but a number," says Ernestine Shepherd. The epitome of physical perfection, it's hard to imagine she was ever the couch potato she says she was at age 56. After she and her sister, Mildred, tried on bathing suits and realized how out of shape she was, she started taking aerobics which graduated to bodybuilding.

Since then she has run nine marathons, won two bodybuilding contests, and was named the Guinness World Record holder for the oldest competitive female body builder in 2010, and 2011 when she was 74.

A retired school administrator, Ernestine has six-pack abs that would be the envy of anyone at any age. But a body like hers doesn't happen overnight. Her regimen begins every morning at 3:00 a.m. to meditate and create a mindset for her workout, followed by a 10-mile run, and then a two-hour strength workout under the tutelage of former Mr. Universe, Yohannie Shambourger.

Phew! Just one of those activities sounds tiring. Yet, she also teaches fitness classes full-time, and trains women at the gym every single day. Tenacious and driven, she has never looked back from that day when she struggled to buy a bathing suit.

Principle:

We have a lot more control over our aging than we believe. Even in mid-life it's possible to dramatically reinvent your physical appearance and health.

Action:

Remember Newton's famous law that states, "A body at rest tends to remain at rest and a body in motion tends to remain in motion," and get started moving today. Referring back to Arthur Berger's theory on the power of the mind, it's never too late to have a mind makeover to create a body makeover!

40

FAUJA SINGH

Since we're on the subject of success after 50 in physical achievements, we can't overlook Fauja Singh who became the world's oldest marathon runner.

Born in 1911, he didn't walk until he was five years old. But once his legs were strong enough he became an avid amateur runner, a habit he kept until his mid-thirties. Then due to tumultuous events and responsibilities, he gave it up for more than 60 years.

Singh had gone through excruciating heartbreak when his son was decapitated during a violent thunderstorm. So he and his family moved to London to help him get over his devastating loss. After losing his wife, his son and his eldest daughter, he decided to return to his passion for running. He was 89-years-old at that time, and ended up participating in many international marathons.

Singh became famous at the age of 93 when he knocked 58 minutes off the previous world's best time for the 90-plus age bracket. Then at the age of 100 he set eight world records for his age group in one day.

Fauja Singh was the first 100-year-old in history to finish a marathon, and carried the Olympic torch in July 2012.

Principle:

Many people give up their passions to follow other paths. But those passions still lie within them, waiting for the proper time to manifest into something tangible. Like Fauja Singh, don't ignore the call of a passion that has been dormant for years, as there may be the most spectacular finish line waiting for you.

Action:

Take time to dig out scrapbooks and memorabilia that contain things you did years ago. Motivational speaker Denis Waitley says the seed for many of our passions were planted in your early years, and it's never too late to harvest one or more of them!

41

WALLACE STEVENS

Although Wallace Stevens (1879-1955) received his education at Harvard and the New York School, and had a life-long career at the Hartford Accident and Indemnity Company, he's mainly known for his contributions to the field of poetry.

His first major publication (four poems from a sequence entitled "Phases" in the November 1914 edition of Poetry) was written at the age of 35, although he had written many poems and sonnets while attending college.

Influenced by Post-Impressionist artist Paul Cézanne, and Expressionist Paul Klee, his first book of poetry titled Harmonium was published in 1923. Continuously inspired by the raw beauty during his trips to Key West, Florida, he wrote two more collections during the 1920s and 1930s, and three more in the 1940s.

Stevens earned the National Book Award for Poetry (twice), and the Pulitzer Prize for Poetry in 1955 shortly before his death.

Principle:

It might seem odd for a Harvard educated insurance salesman to become a poet. But the moral of this story is it's never too late to live the kind of life you want to live.

Action:

Wallace Stevens is a prime example of switching the brain from analytical to creative, and to be successful in both areas if that's what you're determined to do. Don't be afraid to take on something completely new as long as it excites you, presents you with the possibilities for more achievement, and gets you closer to your dreams. It's never too late begin a new career at any age!

42

OSCAR SWAHN

The words "old" and "Olympian" are seldom synonymous. But they describe Oscar Gomer Swahn (1847-1927), a Swedish marksman who won a bronze and two gold medals at the 1908 Olympics in Stockholm when he was 60; gold and bronze medals in 1912 when he was 64; and a silver medal in 1920 when he was 72, which earned him the honor of being the oldest gold medalist in Olympic history.

The best part of the story is the physicality of his competitions: Deer single-shot; running deer single; and double-shot. When other people Swahn's age were basking in the boredom of retirement, he was as active as his counterparts. Just thinking of the events he competed in is enough to make you exhausted!

Principle:

The Olympics are typically viewed as a young person's game, even in events more suitable to older physiques such as marksmanship. But Swahn made it to the Olympics utilizing skill, experience, and a keen and steady eye.

Action:

It's important to keep the competitive spirit going even when you're older. If you've ever met someone who seems young beyond their years, it's often because they retain the competitive spirit of their youth (there are thousands of stories of people who run marathons, climb mountains, white-water raft, play poker or golf).

Competing against others can give you motivation to take action beyond what societal norms would have you be doing at your age. To put this in even more clarity, Swahn was competing just five years before his death in 1927 – a perfect example of it's never too late to do anything you want!

43

FLORA THOMPSON

An author and poet most famous for her Lark Rise to Candleford trilogy, Flora Thompson (1876-1947) stands in contrast to many of the other writers I've discussed. Why? While other writers began their careers and achieved success after 50, Flora achieved her greatest success when she was 62 years old.

After leaving home at the age of 14, she worked as a clerk in the Fringford post office in southern England. In a few years she got a job as an assistant at the Grayshott post office in Hampshire

With a penchant for books, she spent a great deal of time at the Winton library. And in 1911, she won an essay competition in The Ladies Companion for a 300-word essay about Jane Austen.

Flora met her future husband, John, who also worked at the Grayshott post office. Together they would have one daughter and two sons.

After moving to Bournemouth, she wrote essays to augment their income. Her first work, Bog-Myrtle and Peat (a collection of poems), was published in 1921 when she was in her 40s but wasn't very successful.

It was her autobiographical trilogy that finally earned her journalism acclaim: Lark Rise to Candleford published in 1945 (originally published in 1939 as Lark Rise); Over to Candleford (1941); and Candleford Green (1943). Her final work, Still Glides the Stream, was published in 1948 after her death.

Principle:

Flora Thompson didn't let age deter her, nor did she let the failure of her first publication stop her when inspiration found her later in life. The loss of her son caused her great grief. But she kept writing until her death with some of her later works being published posthumously.

Action:

You might wonder how you can replicate Flora Thompson's success. First, don't let the excuse of "I've tried that before" convince you that you're over the hill at 50. Second, if you find those kinds of thoughts flying around your head, remember that she could have used that excuse but successfully ignored it.

It's never too late to write your poetry, pen that novel, write those articles, or even put together a recipe book. The only limitations are your excuses and fear of trying.

44

DORIS EATON TRAVIS

Doris Eaton Travis (1904-2010) appeared on Broadway for the first time as the youngest Ziegfeld girl ever to perform. She was just 14 years old.

After her career on stage and in silent films declined in the late 1930s, she started a second career as an Arthur Murray dance instructor, and as a television personality in Detroit.

She stayed with Arthur Murray for over three decades, during which time she also managed a chain of nearly 20 schools.

At the age of 88, she graduated cum laude from the University of Oklahoma with a degree in history and the distinction as its oldest graduate.

In 1998 at the age of 94, she made Broadway history by appearing at the New Amsterdam Theatre where she tap danced in an AIDS benefit, and became the oldest Ziegfeld girl to perform on stage.

She purchased a 220-acre horse ranch Oklahoma that she operated with her husband, Paul Travis. And at the age of 99 she wrote her memoirs, "Days We Danced: The Story of My Theatrical Family From Florenz Ziegfeld to Arthur Murray." Doris Eaton

Travis made public appearances until days before her passing at age 106.

Principle:

Achievement and failure are purely habits. But those people who consistently push themselves toward seeking achievement are the ones who will succeed. Activity keeps you alive, it keeps you young, and it prevents you from becoming stagnant. Plus, it gives you opportunities to pursue as many passions as possible before you head to that big "stage" in the sky.

Action:

Create a bucket list (a list of life goals) if you don't have one. Check off things as you accomplish them, and constantly refer to it for new adventures until you're 100 or older. It's never too late to "dance like nobody's watching" or on stage in front of an audience.

45

ALFRED WALLIS

Another example of "naïve art" (which is in the same category as Grandma Moses), Alfred Wallis' paintings give no indication to his background.

Wallis (1855-1942) was initially trained as a basketmaker before becoming a mariner in the merchant service in the 1870s.

As a result, he sailed around the North Sea and in the areas surrounding Great Britain.

A pivotal moment in his life was when he married Susan Ward (who was 21 years older). Becoming a stepfather to her five children, Wallis gave up his life at sea in favor of local fishing to help support the family.

When Susan died in 1922, he took up painting at age 67, telling a friend he was doing it for the "company." Self-taught, he painted seascapes from memory. English painters Ben Nicholson and Kit Wood discovered Wallis' paintings after they moved to Cornwall to establish an artist colony. Though the connection would lead to Wallis becoming well-known in London and among influential artist circles, his greatest fame came after his death.

Principle:

Alfred Wallis is an example of a late bloomer who was motivated by a devastating event to create something fresh and of great importance. Many sad moments contain the seeds that can grow to heights we can never imagine. It's never too late use the emotions of a heartbreak or life-altering experience to catapult you into a new life!

Action:

Are you carrying the pain of losing a loved one, a job, or a way of life that can be your motivation? Planting seeds to grow your creativity can be cathartic and a way to heal.

46

MARY WESLEY

Mary Aline Mynors Farmar Wesley (1912-2002) was born in Englefield Green, Surrey, England, into a privileged family. But her books were born much later than that. In fact, her three children's books – Speaking Terms, The Sixth Seal, and Haphazard House – all published before her foray into adult fiction.

Considering they weren't published until Wesley was almost 60, her success as an author is indeed a late-blooming accomplishment. Obviously the books she would contribute to the world would come very late in life.

Mary is a perfect example of someone who never lost her youthful capacity for creative production. Even when she was in her 70s she was still writing at a very rapid rate. Her books came about every year or so, and continued well into the 1990s. It was only when she turned 84 did she stop writing fiction, saying, "If you don't have anything left to say, don't say it."

Later in life Mary consented to a biography being written about her life, but on the condition it wouldn't come out until after she was dead. By the time she passed away at the age of 90, she had written over a dozen published books.

Principle:

Once Mary started writing, her unwavering focus allowed her to be just as prolific as a younger author might be. Bearing in mind that Wesley was in her 70s and 80s when she was penning her novels, the phrase "younger author" can apply to a much broader spectrum of the population.

Action:

It's never too late to be focused and productive in order to turn out creativity. Mary Wesley is a shining example of someone who was able to produce an entire catalogue of work even though she hadn't been writing her entire life.

CASPAR WESSEL

When you think about renowned mathematicians and academics, you most likely think about people who were on the road to greatness at a very young age.

This, however, was not the case with Caspar Wessel (1745-1818), who made his contributions to the field of mathematics in 1799 with his paper, Om directionens analyitske betegning, being published by the Royal Danish Academy of Sciences and Letters.

A Norwegian-Danish mathematician born in Norway, Wessel was the very definition of a late bloomer. After completing secondary school in 1763, he went to Denmark for further studies and acquired the degree of candidatus juris from the University of Copenhagen in 1778.

However, he didn't follow the traditional track as an academician as he was employed as a surveyor and mapmaker for the Danish Royal Academy in 1794 (and 1798 as Royal Inspector of Surveying). One of the maps he drew after he retired had been requested by Napoleon Bonaparte. In 1815 Wessel was made a Knight of the Order of Dannebrog in recognition of his exceptional contribution to surveying.

Wessel's geometric interpretations he had written for the Danish Royal Academy in 1787 were rediscovered in 1806 and then again in 1831. But his findings were not noticed by the mathematical community until 1895. A French translation was published in 1897, and it was not available in English until even much later.

In previous examples we've looked at people who began their contributions to the world over the age of 50. Even though this would be Caspar Wessel's only paper when he was 55, the mathematical world found his contributions worth publishing.

Principle:

You don't have to be a prodigy to publish important scientific or academic work. Similarly, you don't have to have a career in mathematics in order to make a significant contribution to the field. Too many people make the mistake of assuming that because they haven't done anything of any magnitude, they can't accomplish greatness in the future.

Action:

Today people have the Internet where they can post their ideas, so don't be afraid to express yours. Even if they don't earn instant acclaim, it doesn't mean won't to be considered valuable at some point. It's never too late to make your claim to fame!

48

LAURA INGALLS WILDER

Many children's first experience with literature was with the Little House on the Prairie series. Laura Elizabeth Ingalls (1867-1957) was born in Wisconsin, but moved to Kansas and would eventually live in Missouri. Taking a teaching position at around age 16, she eventually settled down with her husband in a cabin and lived the prairie lifestyle she would eventually write about.

Laura's writing started slowly, with writing newspaper columns and periodicals. To help bring money back into their family after the stock market crash in 1929, she approached her daughter, Rose, about collaborating on a book she had toyed with.

Originally called Little House in the Woods, the famous prairie series was first published in 1932 when Laura Ingalls Wilder was 62 years old.

Principle:

Look for opportunities to collaborate with your children. Although historians argue about how much influence Rose had in creating the Little House on the Prairie series with her mother, what's evident is if she hadn't played a role the Prairie

might not exist today. Working with your children while they're young or as adults creates a bond, and shows you're flexible and open-minded.

Action:

The next time someone compliments you on a skill or a talent (such as writing), explore how you can use it in service to others. Enlist your children in the brainstorming process, and research ideas that will allow you to work together. If you've always wanted to write (or have written, but set aside any hopes of writing fiction or non-fiction), this example shows it's never too late to start.

49

WINI YUNKER

Seeking adventure in a big city, Winifred "Wini" Yunker left her small town in Kentucky in her '20s and moved to Washington, D.C.

Landing a job down the street from the White House, she often saw President Kennedy and got caught up in his message to "ask what you can do for your country."

But her hopes to be a part of his new Camelot were dashed when the Peace Corps turned her down because she didn't have enough education.

She eventually moved back to Kentucky and got a job in the clerical pool at a lock company. Wini married, had a son, divorced, and like many single parents struggled to keep things afloat. Studying at nights and on weekends she eventually earned a master's degree from the Patterson School of Diplomacy and International Commerce at the University of Kentucky. She progressed through the lock company, and ended up as the chief assistant to the president.

(To add an extra little tidbit, in 1997 she and 22-year-old son, Joe, rappelled off the scenic cliffs of Red River Gorge in Eastern Kentucky.)

When her career at the company was over, she joined the Peace Corps, saying "I'm ready for a new phase in my life." She was 65 years old when she determined what she 'could do for her country.' In 2000, she went to the former Soviet Union with 30 other volunteers to teach Ukrainians how to run a business in a free-market democracy.

Principle:

The dreams of youth are often interrupted by the responsibilities of life. This doesn't mean you should allow the dream to wither, or give up on it altogether. It just means you need to reset your goals clock in order to achieve it.

Action:

Does your dream have special requirements (like Wini needing a master's degree)? It's never too late to acquire the knowledge or skills you need to achieve your goals. Even if you never use them for that purpose, it'll keep your mind engaged and active.

50

TIM AND NINA ZAGAT

You may have heard of the Zagat Restaurant Survey that includes 70 cities, which over the years has expanded from restaurants to venues including hotels, shopping, music, theaters, golf courses and even airlines.

What was once a hobby for Tim and Nina Zagat became a life-defining pursuit. They first met at Yale, and after graduating became practicing attorneys.

They liked to solicit their friends' reviews on restaurants, and eventually put those observations into compilations and later into comprehensive guides. The first Zagat Survey appeared in 1982 and sold some 7,500 copies, which was a moderate success compared to what the Zagat name would eventually become.

Selling some 40,000 copies in 1986 enabled the Zagats to quit their jobs and focus their efforts full-time on their brand. Nina was nearing almost 50 and Tim was 51. Together they proved that you can find success if you stay focused and pursue your dreams.

Principle:

There are a few principles at work here. First, before the Zagats reached their fifties they were successful lawyers with degrees from Yale Law. They didn't need to pursue anything else, but they enjoyed doing the surveys and capitalized on their knowledge. Second, there's nothing to prevent you from taking similar steps when you've hit the big 5-0.

Action:

If you and your significant other have a mutual interest, think about how you can turn it into something more lucrative. The Zagats took a simple idea like restaurant reviews and turned it into something that made their name famous. It's never too late to take a venture you and your partner have been working on and create a successful empire.

CONCLUSION

WHAT TO MAKE OF ALL THESE STORIES
(AND WHERE TO GO FROM HERE)

"Dance like nobody's watching. Love like you've never been hurt. Sing like nobody's listening. Live like it's heaven on earth."

~MARK TWAIN

The commonality behind all these stories is that people achieved their greatest success after the age of 50. Some achieved success in business. Others in literature, film or politics. And some achieved success early in life, while others were failures or led inconsequential lives.

But the mutual thread is twofold: First, each one of these people could have felt limited by their age, but ignored those negative thoughts. And second, they persisted when they were tempted to quit.

Of course, in some cases not quitting is easy. Grandma Moses probably wouldn't have quit painting even if she never earned more than a few dollars from the sales of her works.

In some cases, not quitting is hard. Can you imagine the stress that must have taken a toll on Winston Churchill or Abraham Lincoln during some of the most tumultuous times in history?

But for everyone in this book, quitting was not an option. Even if they failed in one field they found success in another by changing their strategy and their original path.

Sure, age can be a convenient excuse and sometimes a legitimate obstacle. But quite often it's not your age (a mindset) but your health that can get in the way. There are plenty of young people with bad health problems, and old people who are in great condition.

If you allow people to talk you out of what you want to do because they think you're too old, that's their problem. Your age has little to nothing to do with how they feel about you, as it's usually about what they wouldn't do. Ignore the naysayers and the bubble-bursters as it's your life and you need to live it your way!

The important takeaway from all of this is there's no time like the present. You can't go back to before you were 50. But if you start living your life today in order to achieve your dreams, you still have time to make the most with the skills you have.

As these pages attest, you can have a life beyond anything you can imagine. Wouldn't you love to be doing something that can take your breath away and make you successful? Can you imagine doing what you had really wanted to when you were a child?

So what will it be? Will you let your age determine how you're going to live the rest of your life? Are you going to use it as an excuse for not trying? Are you going to sink into retirement and let the world's expectations of you rule your world?

Or are you going to take a lesson from Harland Sanders who had only a chicken recipe to sell?

What in the heck are you waiting for? It's never too late to make your "recipe" and get selling! Every one of these examples can help "mentor" you. Research them on the Internet or at the library, buy their books, learn how they overcame obstacles, and adapt their mindsets. When the going gets tough, remember how tough it was for them to get going (and did they get going!).

It doesn't even have to be the people in this book. If you know of someone who's willing to be interviewed, contact them and pick their brains. If they live nearby, offer to take them to lunch or dinner and ask as many questions as you can think of. Take notes, and then put them into action.

One of the greatest experiences I ever had was reaching out to John Goddard, the world's number one goal achiever. The friendship we developed, and the wisdom I gained, have been priceless.

And above all, make this your mantra by repeating to yourself over and over, "It's never too late, and I'm never too old!"

So get going and hang in there. I expect to see your name in the news very soon!

For a free book of Napoleon Hill's classic
***Think and Grow Rich,* go to:**
Get-My-Free-Book.net

About the Author

Twelve years ago Vic Johnson was totally unknown in the personal development field. Since that time he's created six of the most popular personal development sites on the Internet. One of them, www.AsAManthinketh.net has given away over 400,000 copies of James Allen's classic book. Three of them are listed in the top 5% of websites in the world (English language).

This success came despite the fact that he and his family were evicted from their home 16 years ago and the next year his last automobile was repossessed. His story of redemption and victory has inspired thousands around the world as he has taught the powerful principles that created incredible wealth in his life and for many others.

Today he serves more than 300,000 subscribers from virtually every country in the world. He's become an internationally known expert in goal-achieving, and has hosted his own TV show, Goals 2 Go, on TSTN.

His book, 13 Secrets of World Class Achievers, is the number one goal-setting book at both the Kindle store and Apple iBookstore.

Another best seller, Day by Day with James Allen, has sold more than 75,000 copies and has been translated into Japanese, Czech, Slovak and Farsi.

Vic's three-day weekend seminar event, Claim Your Power Now, has attracted such icons as Bob Proctor, Jim Rohn, Denis Waitley and many others.

His websites include:

AsAManThinketh.net

Goals2Go.com

GettingRichWitheBooks.com

TheChampionsClub.org

MyDailyInsights.com

VicJohnson.com

ClaimYourPowerNow.com

LaurenzanaPress.com

Other Books by Vic Johnson

How To Write A Book This Weekend, Even If You Flunked English Like I Did

Day by Day with James Allen

Goal Setting: 13 Secrets of World Class Achievers

52 Mondays: The One Year Path To Outrageous Success & Lifelong Happiness

The Magic of Believing: Believe in Yourself and The Universe Is Forced to Believe In You

Self Help Books: The 101 Best Personal Development

How I Created a Six Figure Income Giving Away a Dead Guy's Book

Think and Grow Rich: The Lost Secret

How To Make Extra Money: 100 Perfect Businesses for Part-Time and Retirement Income

Made in the USA
Columbia, SC
01 March 2023